Morgan Leight

QUAGMIRE
PRESS

Pumpkin Jokes

Q: What do you use to fix a cracked pumpkin?
A: A pumpkin patch!

Q: Who helped the mini pumpkin cross the road?
A: The crossing gourd!

Q: What does a pumpkin like to read?
A: Pulp fiction!

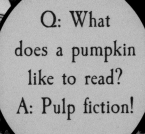

Q: What do you get when you drop a pumpkin?
A: Squash!

Q: What do you get if you divide the circumference of a pumpkin by its diameter?
A: Pumpkin Pi!

Q: What did the orange pumpkin say to the green pumpkin?
A: You look a little sick!

Farm Jokes

Q: What does an evil hen lay?
A: Deviled eggs!

Q: What do you call a chicken that haunts your house?
A: A poultry-geist!

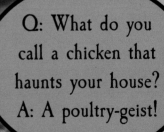

Q: What is a scarecrow's vehicle of choice?
A: An autumn-mobile!

4

Q: Why don't scarecrows eat? A: They're already stuffed!

Q: Why did the scarecrow win an award? A: Because he was outstanding in his field!

Q: What crop did the scarecrow stand over? A: Beets me!

Halloween Food Jokes

Q: What is a ghost's favorite dessert?
A: Boo-berries and I-scream!

Q: Who do ghosts buy cookies from?
A: Ghoul scouts!

Q: What is a vampire's favorite fruit?
A: A blood orange!

Q: What is a ghost's favourite meal?
A: Spook-ghetti!

Q: How do monsters like their eggs?
A: Terror-fried!

Q: What kind of cheese do monsters like best?
A: Monsterella!

7

Jack-o-Lantern Jokes

Q: Why do jack-o-lanterns sit on people's porches?
A: They have no hands to knock on the door!

Q: Why was the jack-o-lantern afraid?
A: He had no guts!

Q: Why do jack-o-lanterns get bad grades?
A: Because they had all their brains scooped out!

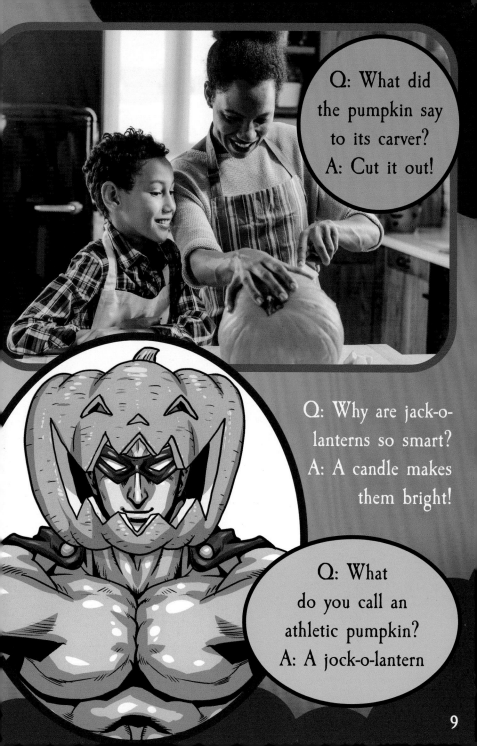

9

Trick-or-Treating Knock Knock Jokes

Knock Knock
Who's there?
Handsome
Handsome who?
Handsome candy
to me.

Knock Knock
Who's there?
Howl
Howl who?
Howl you know
unless you open
the door!

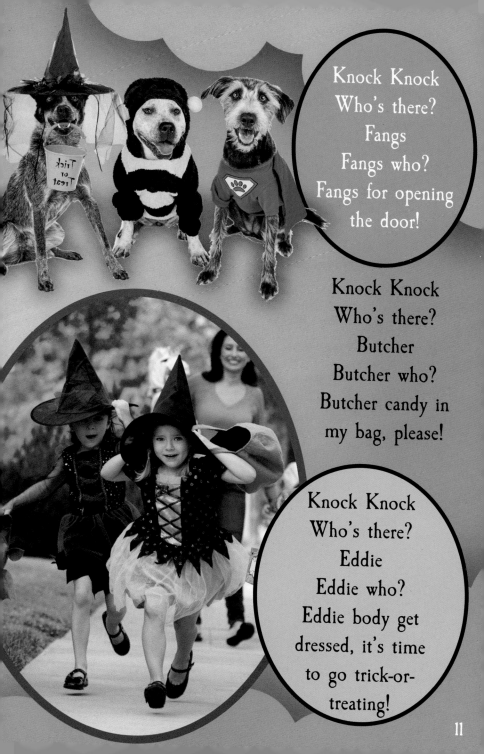

Knock Knock
Who's there?
Fangs
Fangs who?
Fangs for opening
the door!

Knock Knock
Who's there?
Butcher
Butcher who?
Butcher candy in
my bag, please!

Knock Knock
Who's there?
Eddie
Eddie who?
Eddie body get
dressed, it's time
to go trick-or-
treating!

11

Trick-or-Treating Jokes

Q: What did the little boy say when he had to choose between a tricycle and candy?
A: Trike or Treat!

Q: What do birds say on Halloween?
A: Twick or Tweet!

Q: What do hockey players say on Halloween?
A: Hat trick or treat!

More Trick-or-Treating Jokes

Q: Where do werewolves store the candy they get from trick-or-treating?
A: In a were-house!

Q: Where do you find the spookiest Halloween candy to give trick-or-treaters?
A: At the ghost-ery store!

Q: What do witches put on to go trick-or-treating?
A: Mas-scare-a!

Q: What do they do in Minecraft on Halloween?
A: Go trick or creeping!

Q: When do ghosts like to go trick-or-treating?
A: In the moaning!

15

Candy Jokes

Q: What candy do you eat on the playground?
A: Recess pieces!

Q: Why did the M&M go to college?
A: Because he wanted to be one of the Smarties!

Q: Why did the monster do well on his test?
A: Because he ate a lot of Smarties!

Q: What candy is never on time?
A: Choco-late!

Q: What do you call a sheep covered in chocolate?
A: A candy baaa!

Q: Who's in charge of all the candy corn?
A: The kernel!

17

Candy Knock Knock Jokes

Knock Knock
Who's there?
Al
Al who?
Al trade you
a Snickers for
a Kit Kat.

Knock Knock
Who's there?
Diane
Diane who?
Diane to eat
my Halloween
candy!

Knock, Knock
Who's there?
Phillip!
Phillip who?
Phillip my bag
with Halloween
candy, please!

Knock Knock
Who's there?
Aida
Aida who?
Aida lot of candy,
and my tummy
hurts.

Knock Knock
Who's there?
Candy
Candy who?
Candy boy have another
piece of chocolate?

Costume Jokes

Q: Why do superheroes always get the bad guys?
A: Because they're so cape-able!

Q: What happened to the boy who dressed up as half human, half horse for Halloween?
A: He was the centaur of attention!

Q: What do heroes like Spiderman and Ant Man have in common?
A: They bug the villains!

Q: How much did the pirate pay for his earrings?
A: A buccaneer!

Q: What did the pirate say when it snowed on Halloween?
A: Shiver me timbers!

Q: Why are pirate costumes the coolest?
A: They just ARRRRRRRR!

21

Dracula Jokes

Q: Why couldn't Dracula's wife get to sleep?
A: Because of his coffin!

DRACULA

Q: What is Dracula's favourite ice cream flavour?
A: Vein-illa!

Q: Why couldn't Dracula play baseball?
A: He lost his bat!

Q: Where does Dracula keep his money?
A: The blood bank!

Q: How do you join Dracula's fan club?
A: Send your name, address and blood type.

Q: What is it called when Dracula rearranges furniture with his teeth?
A: Fang-shui!

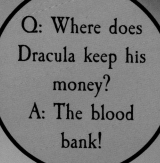

Vampire Jokes

Q: Why don't vampires have more friends?
A: Because they are a pain in the neck!

Q: What kind of tests do vampires give their students?
A: Blood tests!

Q: What did the little vampire say when he went to bed?
A: Turn on the dark, I am afraid of the light!

Q: What is the national holiday for a nation of vampires?
A: Fangs-giving!

Q: What's it called when a vampire has trouble with his house?
A: A grave problem!

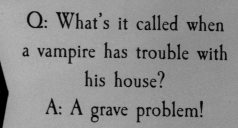

Q: What does a vampire never order at a restaurant?
A: The "stake" sandwich!

Witch Jokes

Q: What does a witch use in her hair?
A: Scare spray!

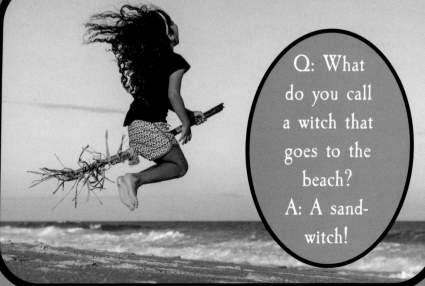

Q: What do you call a witch that goes to the beach?
A: A sand-witch!

Q: Why do witches wear name tags when they get together? A: So they will know which witch is which!

Q: What sound do witches make when they eat cereal? A: Snap, Cackle & Pop!

Q: What do you call witches that live together? A: Broom-mates!

27

More Witch Jokes

Q: What's a witch's favorite subject in school?
A: Spell-ing!

Q: Why don't angry witches ride their brooms?
A: They're afraid they'll fly off the handle.

Q: How many witches does it take to change a light bulb?
A: Just one, but she changes it into a frog!

Q: What do witches race on?
A: Vroom sticks!

Q: Why do witches fly on brooms?
A: Because vacuum cleaners are too heavy!

Q: Why did the witch give up fortune telling?
A: Because there was no future in it!

29

Black Cat Jokes

Q: When is it bad luck to be followed by a black cat? A: When you are a mouse!

Q: What is the official magazine of black cats? A: Good Mousekeeping!

Q: What do you call a black cat surrounded by mice? A: Purr-fectly happy!

Q: What do black cats like to eat on hot days? A: Mice cream cones!

More Black Cat Jokes

Q: What do black cats wear on Halloween night?
A: Paw-jamas!

Q: How did the black cats end their fight?
A: They hissed and made up!

Q: Where does a black cat go if it loses its tail?
A: The re-tail store!

Q: What did the black cat say when the dog ate its Halloween candy?
A: You gotta be kitten me!

trick or treat

Q: Why was the black cat so grumpy?
A: He was in a bad mewd.

Q: Why are black cats so terrible at telling scary stories?
A. Because they have only one tail!

Spider Jokes

Q: What do you call two recently married spiders?
A: Newly-webs!

Q: Why are spiders great web developers?
A: They like finding bugs!

Q: What did the spider say when he broke his web?
A: Darn it!

Q: What did the spider say to the fly on Halloween?
A: The web is the trick, and you are the treat!

Q: What did one spider say to the other?
A: Time is fun when you're having flies!

Skeleton Jokes

Q: Why didn't the little skeleton go to school?
A: His heart wasn't in it!

Q: What instrument does a skeleton play?
A: The trom-bone!

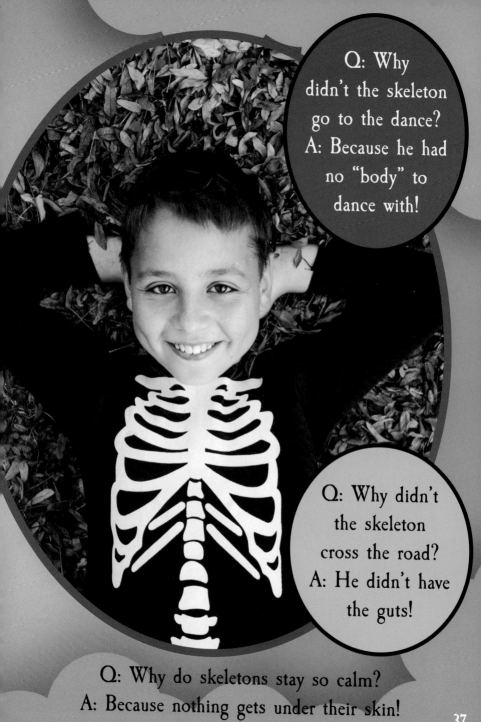

Q: Why didn't the skeleton go to the dance?
A: Because he had no "body" to dance with!

Q: Why didn't the skeleton cross the road?
A: He didn't have the guts!

Q: Why do skeletons stay so calm?
A: Because nothing gets under their skin!

37

More Skeleton Jokes

Q: What do skeletons fly around in?
A: A scareplane or a skelecopter!

Q: Why did the skeleton climb up the tree?
A: Because a dog was after his bones!

Q: Why did the little skeleton laugh at the joke?
A: Because he thought it was humerus!

Q: How do you make a skeleton laugh? A: Tickle her funny bone!

Q: How did the skeleton know what would happen next? A: He could feel it in his bones!

Q: What do you call a lie told by a skeleton? A: A little fib-ula

Still More Skeleton Jokes

Q: Where did the skeleton keep his pet bird?
A: In his rib cage!

Q: Why didn't the skeleton eat spicy food?
A: He didn't have the stomach for it!

Q: Why did the skeleton cross the road?
A: To go to the body shop

Q: What do you call a skeleton who uses the doorbell?
A: A dead ringer!

Q: Who is the most famous skeleton detective?
A: Sherlock Bones

Q: What do skeletons say before they begin eating?
A: "Bone" Appetit!

Cemetery Jokes

Q: Why did the black cat cross the cemetery?
A: Claws it wanted to!

Q: Did you hear about the untidy cemetery?
A: You wouldn't want to be caught dead in there!

Q: Why is a cemetery a great place to write a story?
A: Because there are so many plots there!

Q: Why do people hate driving in a cemetery?
A: The roads are all dead ends!

Haunted House Jokes

Q: What goes around
a haunted house and never stops?
A: A fence!

Q: What room does
a ghost not enter?
A: The living room!

Q: How do ghosts
go from floor to floor?
A: By scare-case!

Q: What happened to the man
who didn't pay his exorcist?
A: The house was repossessed!

Q: What was
in the stable
at the haunted
farmhouse?
A: Night mares!

Spooky Knock Knock Jokes

Knock Knock
Who's there?
Ivan
Ivan who?
Ivan to suck your blood!

Knock Knock
Who's there?
Ice cream
Ice cream who?
Ice cream
every time
I see a ghost!

Knock Knock
Who's there?
Boo
Boo who?
Don't cry! I didn't mean
to scare you!

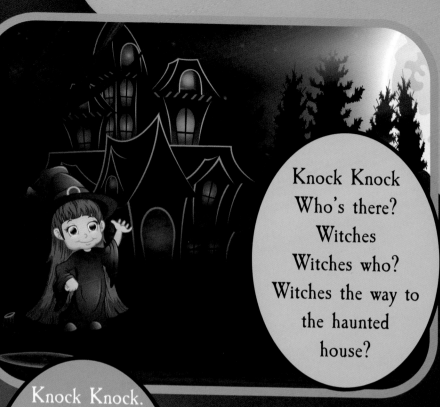

Knock Knock
Who's there?
Witches
Witches who?
Witches the way to
the haunted
house?

Knock Knock.
Who's there?
Tad
Tad who?
Tad house is
haunted. Don't
trick or treat
there!

Ghost Jokes

Q: What game do young ghosts love to play?
A: Hide and shriek!

Q: What did the mother ghost say to her littlest ghost as they drove down the street?
A: Buckle your sheet belt!

BOO!

Q: Where do baby ghosts go during the day?
A: Day-scare centers!

Q: Where do ghosts like to travel on vacation?
A: The Dead Sea!

Q: What is a baby ghost's favorite game?
A: Peek-a-BOO!

Q: What is a spook's favorite amusement ride?
A: A roller-ghoster!

More Ghost Jokes

Q: Where do
fashionable
ghosts shop?
A: Boo-tiques!

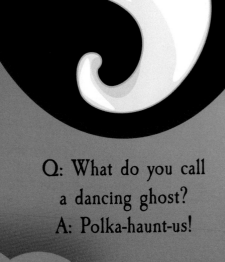

Q: Who did
the ghost invite
to his party?
A: Any old
friend he could
dig up!

Q: What do you call
a dancing ghost?
A: Polka-haunt-us!

Q: What do ghosts wear when their eyesight gets blurry?
A: Spook-tacles!

Q: What day do ghosts do their howling?
A: On Moan-day!

Q: On which day are ghosts most scary?
A: Fright-day!

Still More Ghost Jokes

Q: What happens when a ghost gets lost in the fog?
Q: He is mist.

Q: Why do ghosts hate when it rains on Halloween?
A: It dampens their spirits!

Q: What is a ghost's nose full of?
A: Booooooogers!

Q: What did one ghost say to the other? A: Get a life!

Q: What position does a ghost play in hockey?
Q: Ghoulie!

Q: Why are ghosts so bad at telling lies? A: Because you can see right through them!

53

Demon Jokes

Q: How do devils show you things?
A: They demonstrate them!

Q: What did the demon do when he got a new house?
A: He had a house burning party!

Q: Who is the fastest devil?
A: The speed demon!

Q: Why do demons and ghouls get along so well?
A: Because demons are a ghoul's best friend!

Q: When do demons wash their clothes?
A: At the end of demonth!

Q: What do devils drink at Halloween parties?
A: Demonade!

Monster Jokes

Q: What monster plays tricks on Halloween?
A: Prank-enstein!

Q: Why did the cyclops give up teaching?
A: Because she only had one pupil!

Q: What did the werewolf eat after his teeth cleaning?
A: The dentist!

Q: What did the monster say to his victim?
A: It's been nice gnawing you!

Q: Did you hear about the monster who ate his own house?
A: He was homesick!

Q: How do monsters tell their future?
A: They read their HORROR-scope!

More Monster Jokes

Q: Why was there thunder and lightning inside the laboratory?
A: Because Dr. Frankenstein and Igor were brain-"storming"!

Q: What's big, scary and has three wheels?
A: A monster riding a tricycle!

Q: Why did the monster eat bullets?
A: She wanted her hair to grow out in bangs!

Q: Who is the best dancer at the monster party?
A: The Boogie Man!

Q: What goes "Ha-ha-ha-ha!" right before a big crash and more laughing?
A: A monster laughing it's head off!

Q: What's even scarier than a monster?
A: A mom-ster!

Mummy Jokes

Q: What kind of music do mummies love?
A: Wrap music!

Q: Why don't mummies have time for fun?
A: They are too wrapped up in their work!

Q: Why didn't the mummy have any friends?
A: He was too wrapped up in himself!

Q: Why don't mummies take vacations?
A: They're afraid they'll relax and unwind!

Q: Why was the mummy so tense?
A: He was all wound up!

Q: Why do mummies love Halloween?
A: All the free candy wrappers!

Zombie Jokes

Q: Why did the zombie skip school?
A: He felt rotten!

Q: Where does the zombie live?
A: On a dead-end street!

Q: What's a zombie's favorite cereal?
A: Rice Creepies!

Q: What is a zombie's favorite thing to eat?
A: Brain food!

Q: What did the baby zombie want for her birthday?
A: A deady bear!

The Publisher: KidsWorld Books

Library and Archives Canada Cataloguing in Publication

Library and Archives Canada Cataloguing in Publication

Title: Halloween jokes for kids / Morgan Leight.

Names: Leight, Morgan, author.

Identifiers: Canadiana (print) 20210271752 | Canadiana (ebook) 20210271760 | ISBN 9781926695495 (softcover) | ISBN 9781926695501 (PDF)

Subjects: LCSH: Halloween—Juvenile humor. | LCGFT: Humor.

Classification: LCC PN6178.C3 L45 2021 | DDC jC818/.602—dc23

Front cover: From Getty Images, Dreamcreation.
Back Cover: From Getty Images, sabelskaya, GlobalP, Roberto Scandola/the8monkey, TatianaNikulina.

Photo credits: From Getty Images, _LeS_, 39b; ~UserGI15613517, 37; adogslifephoto, 11a, 33b; alex5248, 5a; alexei_tm, 55a; ALINA-, 59a; AndreaObzerova, 26a; angkritth, 22a; AnnaStills, 53a; Ariel Skelley, 5b; arinahabich, 8a; Arleevector, 29a; Astrobobo, 29b; Best Content Production Group, 45a; Beto_Junior, 26b; brozova, 16b; Capuski, 4b; Chinga_11, 23a; Choreograph, 8b; ChrisGorgio, 56b; damedeeso, 13a; DebbiSmirnoff, 23b; denis_pc, 49a; Drawkman, 57a; Dualororua, 47a; duh84, 63a; Elena Bondarenko, 31a; evgenyatamanenko, 2a, 25a, 35b, 38b, 59b; FabVietnam_Photography, 17a; FamVeld, 41a; fireflamenco, 48b; fotostok_pdv, 15a; Giuseppe Ramos, 42a; GlobalP, 30, 32b; GreenArtPhotography, 7a; Halfpoint, 16a; happy_lark, 6b; Hatcha, 46; hermandesign2015, 56a; HitToon, 17b, 48a; ia_64, 62; IndigoLT, 20a; jenifoto, 13b; JenniferRuch, 43a; Ju Photographer, 18a; Jupiterimages, 19a; jwblinn, 34b; Kagenmi, 12b; kali9, 61b; Konoplytska, 2b; KuznetsovDmitry, 39a; Lordn, 9a; Lucian3D, 14b; Lynne Mitchell, 14a; marcduf, 40a; maroonich, 7b; MaryValery, 42b; masaya itagaki, 9b; McIninch, 54a; mdmilliman, 12a; Mimosa Studio, 36b; monkeybusinessimages, 11b; MorozVyacheslav, 24; NataliaDeriabina, 3a; Olga Trofimova, 51b; orensila, 31b; Paffy69, 21; Pavel Kanaplitski, 36c; Pavel Naumov, 20b; PavelVinnik, 45b; PCH-Vector, 44; petrenkod, 3b; Pixland, 19b; Popmarleo, 57b; Rawpixel, 10b; RekaReka, 25b; Remains, 52; Rezeda Safina, 6a; Roberto Scandola/the8monkey, 40b; rudall30, 60; sabelskaya, 22b, 60; Sadeugra, 18b; SbytovaMN, 28b, 36a; Sergey Nazarov, 28a; SeventyFour, 15b, 27; Silvia Saez, 55b; stefanamer, 41b; Svetlana Zybina, 34a; TatianaNikulina, 54b; tcrawford78, 58, 61a; thanaphiphat, 43b; Tigatelu, 38a; Tijana87, 10a; Tomacco, 49b; treemouse, 33a; Ulyana Petukhova, 47b; Ulza, 35a; Umkarra, 50; VeraPetruk, 53b; Vivienstock, 32a; Vladislav Nosick, 4a; worldofvector, 51a; yayayoyo, 63b.

We acknowledge the financial support of the Government of Canada.
Nous reconnaissons l'appui financier du gouvernement du Canada.

Funded by the Government of Canada
Financé par le gouvernement du Canada | Canadä

PC: 38-1